© 2022 Sunbird Books, an imprint of Phoenix International Publications, Inc.
8501 West Higgins Road   34 Seymour Street   Heimhuder Straße 81
Chicago, Illinois 60631   London W1H 7JE   20148 Hamburg

www.sunbirdkidsbooks.com

Sunbird Books and the colophon are trademarks of Phoenix International Publications, Inc.

Library of Congress Control Number: 2021938042

ISBN: 978-1-5037-6242-8 Printed in China

The art for this book was rendered digitally.
Text set in Charter BT Pro.

IT'S HER STORY
AMELIA EARHART

Written by Kim Moldofsky
Illustrated by Alan Brown

sunbird books

Amelia Earhart led a life of daring adventures! Born in 1897, she grew up during the early years of flight and became a record-breaking pilot known around the world.

There is more to life than being a passenger!

In 1928, Amelia was a social worker helping immigrant families and flying whenever she could. She was one of the few women with a pilot's license.

Miss Earhart, you have an urgent phone call.

Would you like to make aviation history?

Publisher G.P. Putnam interviewed Amelia.

You'll be the first woman to fly the Atlantic!

A dream!

Let's talk details.

Amelia would be named the flight commander, but Wilmer Stultz would actually fly the plane.

Stultz gets $20,000 as pilot.

You'll need to write articles to help pay for the trip.

Amelia and her younger sister, Muriel, spent their early childhood living with their grandparents. Their father's job as a railroad lawyer kept their parents on the move.

Amelia and Muriel were allowed to play freely.

In quiet moments, Amelia filled her head with grand adventures.

George Eliot

THACKERAY

Black Beauty

Oliver Twist

Harper's Young People

She liked learning about chemistry and physics, and playing sports.

BASKETBALL: DANGEROUS FOR GIRLS

Harriet Quimby: 1st Woman Pilot in U.S.A.

Mom, watch me score!

After high school, Amelia attended Pennsylvania's Ogontz School for Young Ladies.

At Christmas, she visited Muriel at school in Toronto.

The Great War is taking a terrible toll on soldiers. I must help them.

During World War I, Amelia left the Ogontz School to volunteer as a nurse's aide.

Flying is the cat's meow. Wait till you see the upcoming air show.

Everyone flooded the streets to celebrate Armistice Day, the end of the First World War, on November 11, 1918.

WAR ENDS
Wild Day Begins
November 11, 1918

Ready to move on, Amelia reunited with her parents at their new home in Los Angeles, California.

Hi, Mom! Hi, Dad!

And in 1920, at the Winter Air Tournament in Long Beach, she found her next adventure.

I'm going to do *that*.

I want to fly! Buy me a ride?

Frank Hawks, a record-breaking aviator, took Amelia on her first airplane ride. He didn't know she would soon break records, too.

I *must* fly again.

We just can't afford flying lessons.

I'm going to be a pilot. I'll earn the money.

First women vote, now they fly!

This job is wearing me out, but I'll do what it takes to keep flying.

In 1921, Amelia signed up for lessons with Neta Snook, the only female flight instructor around.

Will you teach me?

Before Amelia took to the sky, Neta explained the controls to monitor safe flying.

That one tells you how fast you're going.

Early airplanes were unreliable. Flight training included many stunt-like moves to help in emergency landings.

Neta used a rubber mallet to tap students on the head and bring them back to their senses if they froze in fear.

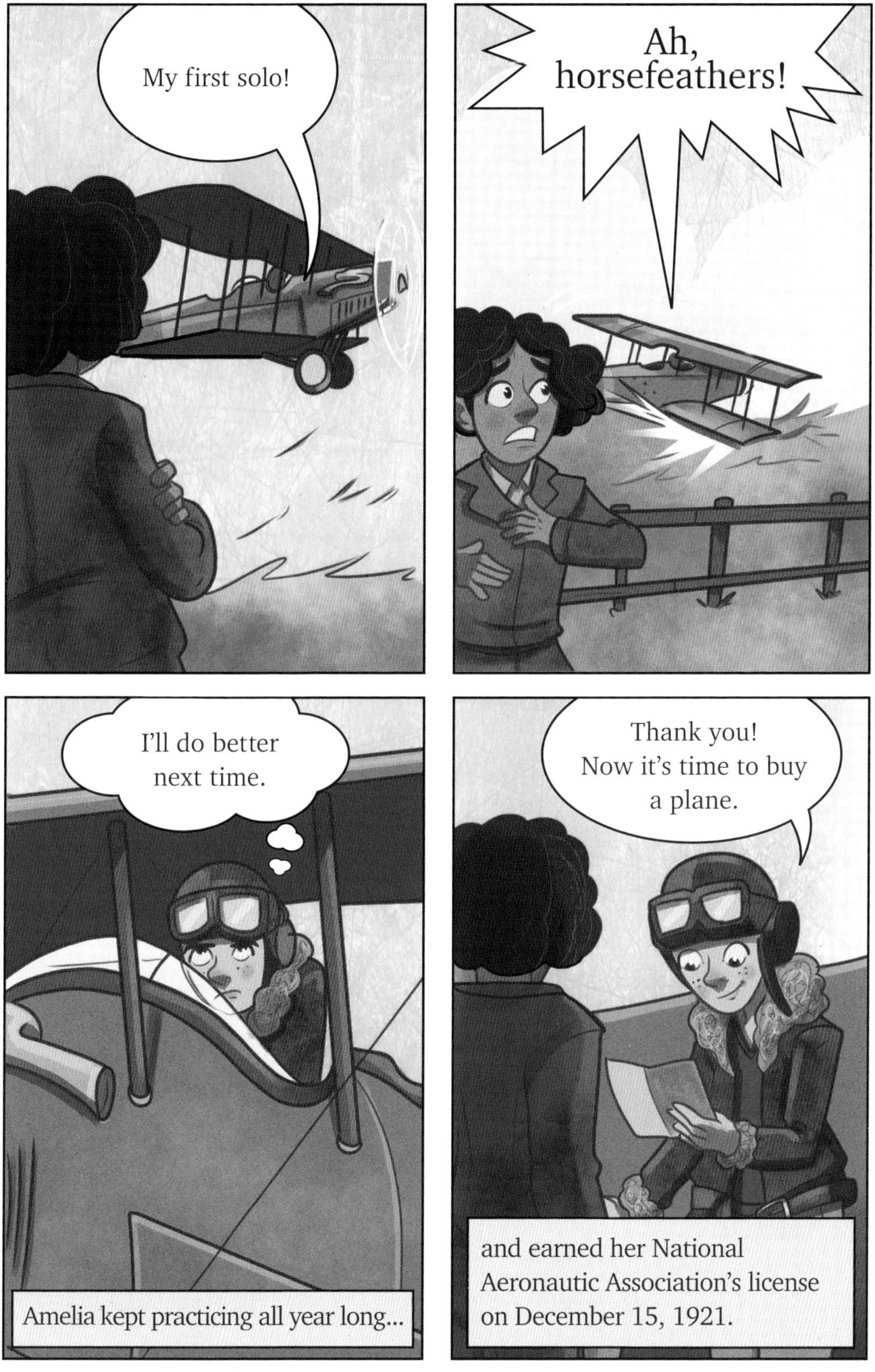
My first solo!
Ah, horsefeathers!
I'll do better next time.
Amelia kept practicing all year long...
Thank you! Now it's time to buy a plane.
and earned her National Aeronautic Association's license on December 15, 1921.

Neta taught Amelia how to drive a car, which was also uncommon for women at that time.

Less fun than flying, but still the bee's knees!

Amelia took many jobs to save for a plane. She built a lifelong habit of working hard to pay for her adventures.

Thanks, Mom—and Muriel—for supporting my dream.

Her first airplane, a secondhand Kinner Airster, cost $2,000.

Behold, the *Canary*!

In 1922, as a new flier, Amelia took the *Canary* up to 14,000 feet, setting a world altitude record for female pilots.

In 1923, she became the 16th woman in the world to earn a pilot's license from the *Fédération Aéronautique Internationale*.

Grounded by sinus problems in 1924, Amelia sold her plane, bought a car, and drove to Boston with her mother.

Yahoo!

She started to dream big again in 1927, when Charles Lindbergh completed his solo flight across the Atlantic Ocean.

And in 1928...

Would you like to make aviation history?

Amelia intended to be the first woman to fly across the Atlantic.

Preparations for record-breaking flights were done in secret. Amelia was kept away from the hangar to avoid attention.

On June 17, 1928, the *Friendship* left Newfoundland, Canada, bound for Ireland.

Here we go!

We're "flying blind."

JUNE 17, 1928. 5,000 FT. A MOUNTAIN OF CLOUDS.

Cloudy weather meant Stultz piloted using instrument readings instead of visual cues.

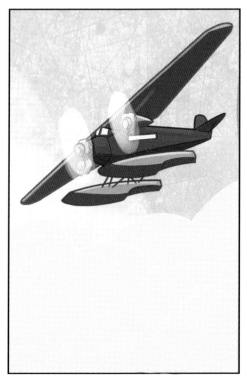

Can you read me?

Low fuel. No radio contact. We're in a pickle.

After 18 hours, the crew thought they were approaching Ireland, but they couldn't be sure because the radio had broken.

We must make contact with that ship.

Here's a trick I learned from Ruth. I'll try to hit the ship's deck!

S.O.S.

Amelia's colleague Ruth Elder had attempted to pilot a transatlantic flight months earlier. Her trip ended with an emergency ocean landing.

Amelia's note missed the target, so Stultz kept on flying.

The *Friendship* crew passed Ireland due to the clouds and lack of radio contact.

On June 18, they landed in Burry Port, Wales—134 miles east of their target. The flight took 20 hours and 49 minutes.

The townspeople were surprised by the unexpected visitors!

Crowds loved the flying trio wherever they went—Wales, London, New York, and across the United States.

What was it like to pilot the plane?

What's your next adventure?

Stultz piloted... I was just baggage.

I'll definitely have more adventures.

G.P. Putnam, who brought Amelia into the *Friendship* crew, now managed her career.

You've got fan mail!

We must keep you in the public eye.

Whatever it takes to make new aviation records.

Smile with your mouth closed to hide your tooth gap.

Enunciate when you speak.

Your posture should suggest confidence.

Be kind to reporters.

To raise money, Amelia gave lectures in more than 30 cities while writing a book. She also appeared in many advertisements.

Amelia bought a secondhand Avro Avian in London. She hoped to take a quiet trip to California for the women's air races.

Buckle in!

But reporters were everywhere!

Aw, applesauce!

A group of 20 determined pilots joined the first national women's race from Santa Monica, California, to Cleveland, Ohio.

1929 Women's Air Derby

The Air Derby planners had concerns.

The 2,000-mile flight race is too difficult for ladies.

Require them to have a man aboard.

If we can't fly and navigate our own course, none of us will enter.

In the end, the women flew without men, but agreed to overnight stops.

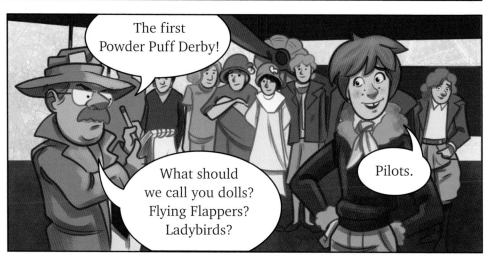

The first Powder Puff Derby!

What should we call you dolls? Flying Flappers? Ladybirds?

Pilots.

Of the 20 fliers, 15 arrived in Cleveland, a higher percentage than had finished in any men's derby to date. Amelia finished third.

It's time to organize.

We want to compete in coed races.

Soon after, 99 women formed a group to support and promote women in aviation. This organization is still active today.

Amelia wrote a monthly magazine column and worked at two new airlines. She encouraged people, especially women, to take flight.

Try Flying Yourself

Amelia Earhart

The Great Depression hurt aviation, but Amelia's career kept growing. She even bought a powerful Lockheed 5B Vega.

My *Little Red Bus.*

In 1930, Amelia was the fourth woman to receive a U.S. transport pilot's license. She also set a new women's world record for flying speed: 181.18 miles per hour.

Marry me. We're a crackerjack team!

Alright, let's do it.

Amelia married G.P. on February 7, 1931. She told the judge she would remain Miss Earhart, not Mrs. Putnam.

Here's to a life of adventure!

Soon after, Amelia set an altitude record of 18,415 feet in a Pitcairn Autogiro, a helicopter-like airplane.

As the first woman to fly cross-country in an autogiro, she planned to prove its safety.

She crashed the aircraft twice. But that didn't stop her.

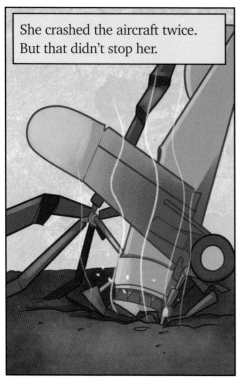

Would you mind if I flew across the Atlantic?

Solo—as the pilot this time, not a passenger.

My life will depend on using these instruments to "fly blind" through clouds and storms.

On May 20, 1932, Amelia departed, alone, from Newfoundland, Canada, headed to Paris.

Do you think I can make it?

You bet.

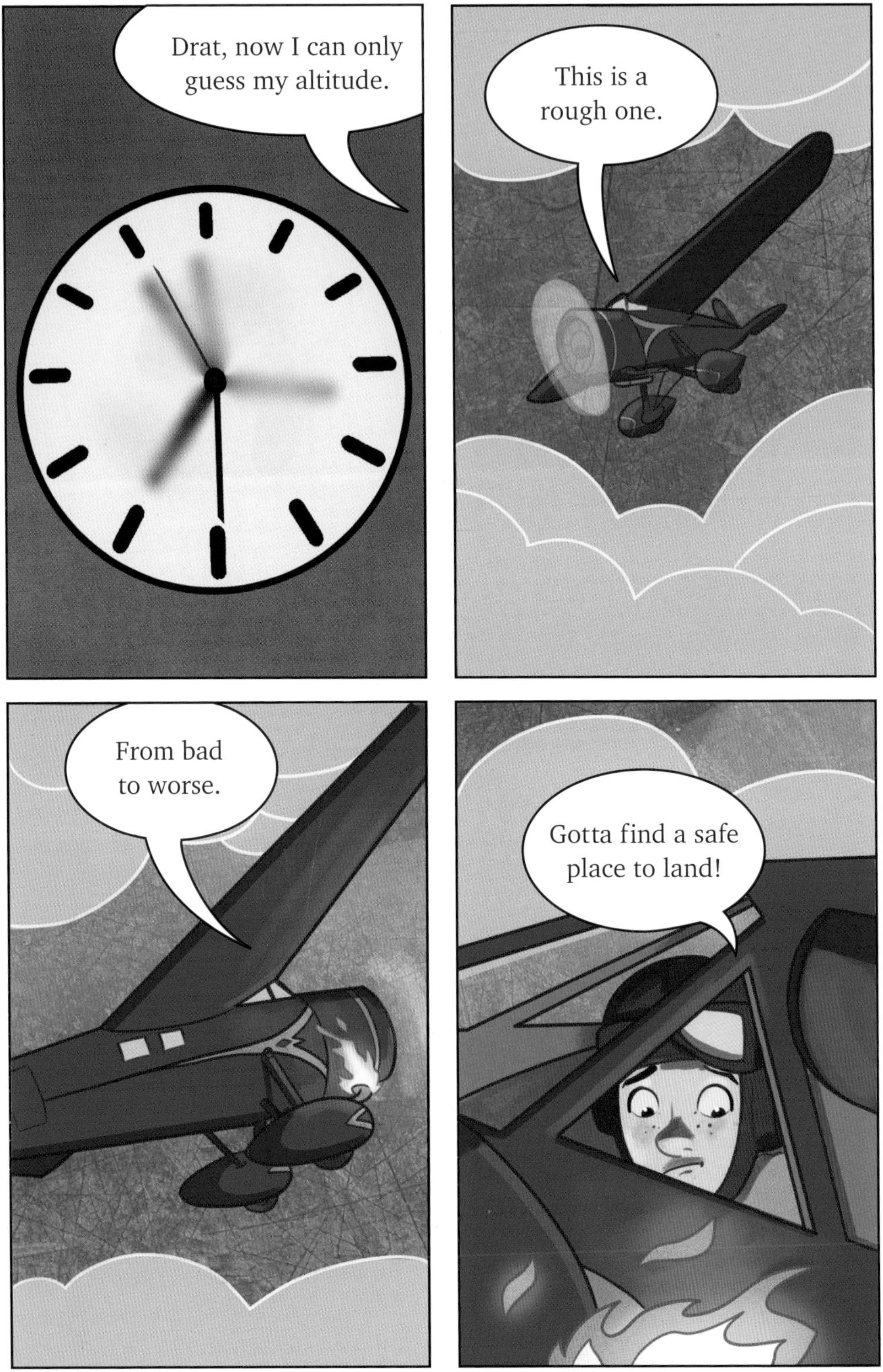
Drat, now I can only guess my altitude.
This is a rough one.
From bad to worse.
Gotta find a safe place to land!

Her record-breaking flight landed in Londonderry, Northern Ireland, 15 hours after take-off.

Amelia was honored around the world. She danced with princes and dined with presidents and prime ministers.

THE CLEVELAND NEWS

AMELIA LANDS ON IRISH COAST

Everyone has an Atlantic to fly. Fly it!

Mrs. Putnam has shown the possibilities of the human spirit.

Ahem, that's *Miss Earhart*. Thank you, President Hoover!

In 1932, Amelia set two more records: top speed and first women's transcontinental solo nonstop flight.

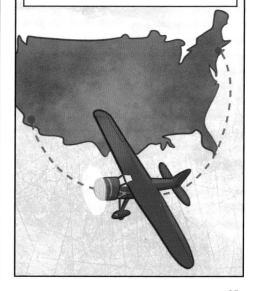

Amelia returned to Washington, D.C., and used her fame to support equality for women.

President Hoover, I stand with the National Woman's Party in hoping for speedy passage of the Equal Rights Amendment.

In the spring of 1933, Amelia snuck First Lady Eleanor Roosevelt away from a party for a quick flight. They returned in time for dessert.

To fund more adventures, Amelia launched a luggage line and a women's clothing line featuring her designs.

DESIGNED BY

Amelia Earhart

Flying from Honolulu to Oakland, California, in 1935, Amelia became the first person to solo both the Atlantic and Pacific Oceans.

Aloha, Honolulu!

She received a hero's welcome.

Later that year, Amelia joined Purdue University's Center for Careers for Women as a consultant and aeronautics adviser.

You deserve exciting careers! First career, *then* marriage.

The Purdue Research Foundation funded Amelia's purchase of a twin-engine Lockheed 10-E Electra.

Thank you for your support. This plane has so much technology, it's practically a flying laboratory.

Amelia brought her new plane to the 1936 air races, where the women finally competed with men.

5th place. Not my best...

but at least *women* won first place.

The race was disappointing. How about another exciting flight— *around the world?!*

Her first attempt at circumnavigation failed.

AMELIA'S PLANE CRASHES

Amelia and her navigator, Fred Noonan, made a new plan.

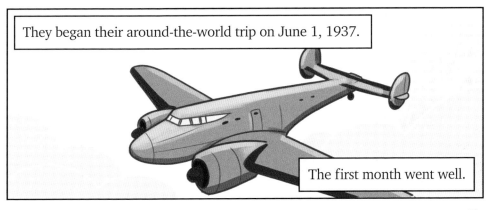

They began their around-the-world trip on June 1, 1937.

The first month went well.

Things changed on July 2, 1937, when they left Lae, Papua New Guinea, for tiny Howland Island.

The U.S. Coast Guard *Itasca* was ready to help navigate the plane to its target.

5:45 AM and 100 miles out.

7:30 AM

We must be near, but can't see you. Fuel is running low. Unable to reach you by radio.

That was her last radio transmission.

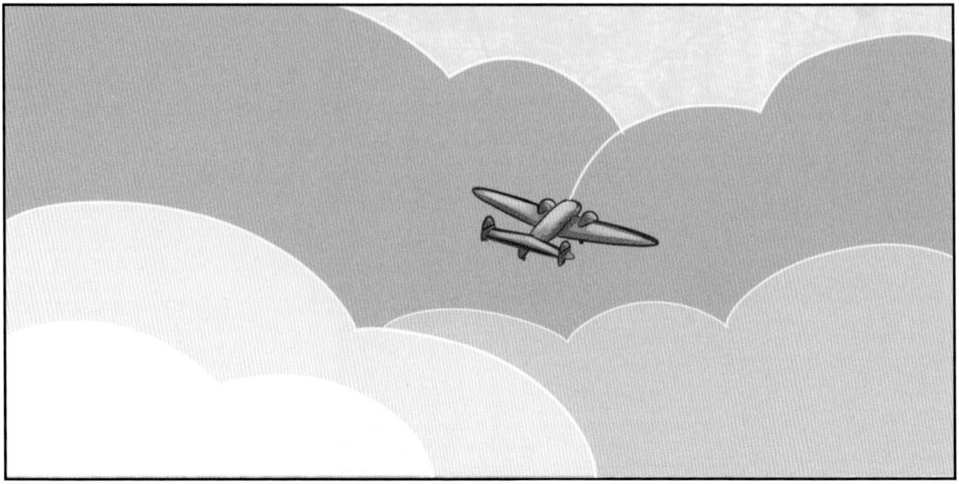

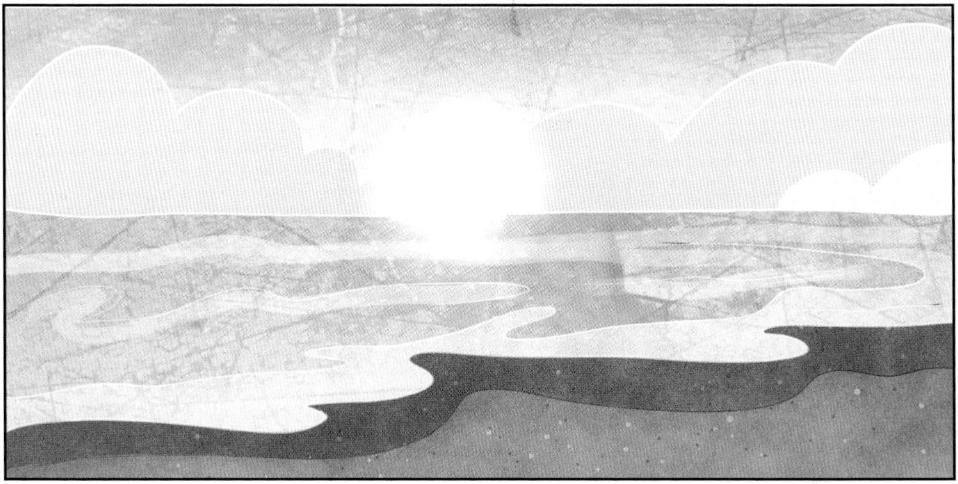

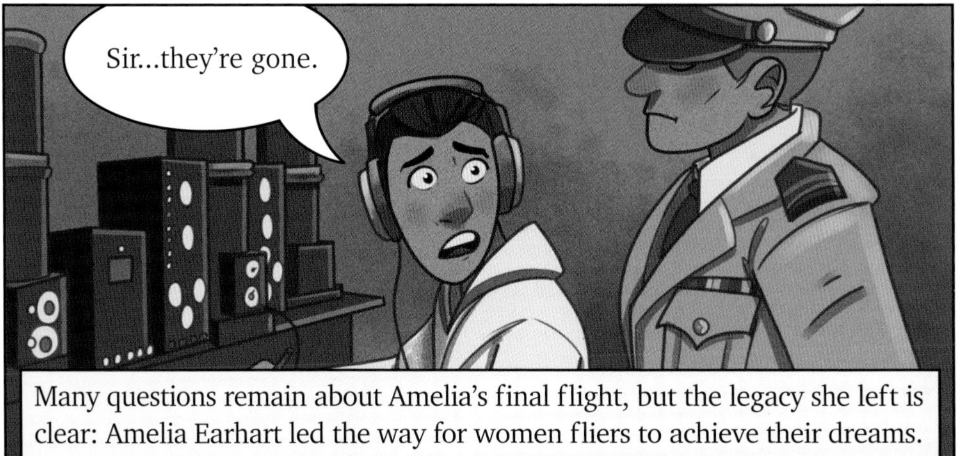

Sir...they're gone.
Many questions remain about Amelia's final flight, but the legacy she left is clear: Amelia Earhart led the way for women fliers to achieve their dreams.

Aim for the Stars

Jeanne M. Holm
First female one-star general of the U.S. Air Force

Ellen Ochoa
First Latina astronaut in space

Mae Jemison
First Black woman astronaut, first Black woman in space

Mary Golda Ross
First Native American aerospace engineer

Bessie Coleman
First Black woman to get a pilot's license

Katherine Sui Fun Cheung
First licensed Asian American pilot

43

Amelia lived a courageous life and inspired so many others to believe, as she did, that

"ADVENTURE
IS WORTHWHILE IN ITSELF."

Kim Moldofsky is an all-around creative person and lifelong learner with a penchant for adventure. Inspired by Amelia, she recently flew in a restored 1929 biplane. In turn, Kim has inspired a generation of STEM kids through her website, *The Maker Mom*. This is her first book.

Alan Brown lives and works as a children's book illustrator on the North Coast of England. When he's not drawing adventures and mysteries, he can be found out and about having adventures and solving mysteries with his wife, sons, and fuzzball companion Otto the Cockapoo.

"WOMEN MUST TRY TO DO THINGS
AS MEN HAVE TRIED. WHERE THEY
FAIL, THEIR FAILURE MUST BE BUT
A CHALLENGE TO OTHERS."